Everything You Need to Know About

STD

Sexually Transmitted Disease

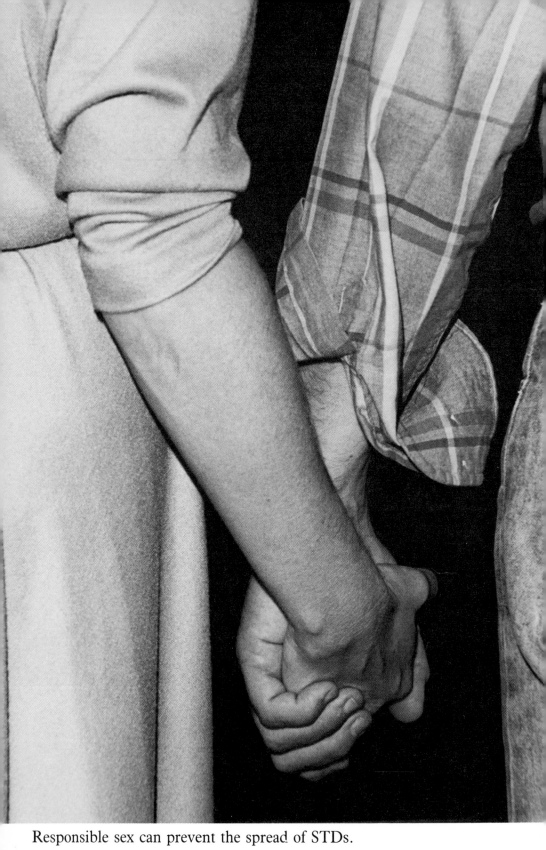

Responsible sex can prevent the spread of STDs.

Everything You Need to Know About

STD
Sexually Transmitted
Disease

Samuel G. Woods

Laura Diskavich, M.S., R.N.C.
Technical Consultant

Series Editor: Evan Stark, Ph.D.

THE ROSEN PUBLISHING GROUP, INC.
NEW YORK

Published in 1990 by The Rosen Publishing Group, Inc.
29 East 21st Street, New York City, New York 10010

First Edition
Copyright 1990 by The Rosen Publishing Group, Inc.

Manufactured in the United States of America.

Library of Congress Cataloging-in-Publication Data

Woods, Samuel G.
    Everything you need to know about STD (sexually transmitted
diseases)/Samuel G. Woods.
    (The Need to know library)
    Includes bibliographical references.
    Index.
    Summary: Describes sexually transmitted diseases, including AIDS,
syphilis, gonorrhea, and genital herpes, and discusses their medical
dangers and where to get help.
    ISBN 0-8239-1010-5
    I. Title. II. Series.
RC200.W66   1989
616.95′1—dc20   89-70118
                                                CIP
                                                  AC

Contents

Introduction

Many people are embarassed by serious talk about sex. It is a very private subject. And it is very personal. That is why most teenagers don't talk about sex with adults. Many teenagers don't even talk about it with each other. There are many things about sex that people should talk about. Talking and listening are important to learning. And it is important to learn about sexually transmitted diseases.

Most sexually transmitted diseases are very dangerous. Some can cause death. Others can hurt you for the rest of your life. And most people get sexually transmitted diseases because they don't know about them. They don't know how a person gets these diseases. They don't know what the signs are.

Most people don't even know that most of these diseases can *easily be prevented*. That is why it is important for everyone to learn about sexually transmitted diseases. It is also important for teenagers and adults to discuss the facts about the diseases together. Preventing these diseases is *so important* that it's worth a little embarrassment.

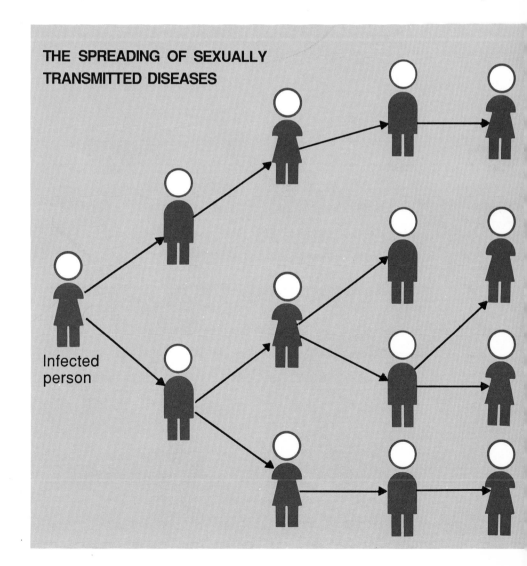

THE SPREADING OF SEXUALLY TRANSMITTED DISEASES

Infected person

Today, people are more aware of sexually transmitted diseases than they were five or ten years ago. Public messages about "safer sex" and using condoms are very common today. You can see ads about condoms and AIDS on the subway or bus and in the newspapers. Most people are now very aware of AIDS.

There are a number of other diseases you can get when you have sex. And these diseases have not been talked about very much on the radio, on TV, or in the newspapers. AIDS has been getting all the attention. In this book we will discuss many of the other sexually transmitted diseases.

If you think you may have a sexually transmitted disease, you probably feel embarrassed. You may think you are the only one who has it. You may feel very alone. But you are not alone. Each day about 2,000 teens get gonorrhea (gon-or-ee-ah) or syphilis (sif-ill-is). Gonorrhea is one of the most common sexually transmitted diseases.

AIDS is the most talked-about sexually transmitted disease. It has infected tens of thousands of people. Some experts think that almost 10 million Americans will carry the virus by 1991.

Why do so many people have sexually transmitted diseases? One reason is that more young people are having sex at an early age. And many young people have sex with one partner and then with another. This increases the chances that they will have sexual contact with an infected partner.

Many young people do not know the facts about sex and diseases that are sexually transmitted. Many teens feel too embarrassed to ask for help about sex. Puberty is a tough time. Teens have many confusing feelings about sex during puberty. Often they are afraid to ask questions.

Many people who have a sexually transmitted disease don't know that they have it. These people then continue to have sex. And they spread the disease to their partners.

Another reason there are so many cases is because many people who know they have a disease don't do enough to cure it. They continue to have sex with others before they are cured. So they spread the disease.

In this book you will learn the facts about sexually transmitted diseases. We will talk about sex and our bodies. You will learn about signs of diseases, and how to spot them early. We will talk about preventing these diseases. And we will discuss how to have "safer sex." If, and when, you decide to have sex you will want to protect yourself and your partner.

You will also learn that there is no reason to be embarrassed. These diseases are common. Most can be cured. You will see that only one thing is more dangerous than getting these diseases—not knowing about them.

Getting the facts about health risks is important.

Chapter 1

Facts About Sexually Transmitted Diseases

Sexually transmitted diseases are called STDs. There are many kinds of STDs. They all share many things. In this chapter we will talk about the ways that all the STDs are alike.

Sexually transmitted diseases are also called venereal diseases. VD is the common name for venereal disease. All venereal diseases are transmitted during sex or close body contact.

Among all the STDs, syphilis, gonorrhea, genital herpes, chlamydia (cla-mid-ee-ah), venereal warts, and AIDS are the most common. They are the most dangerous. Especially if they are not tended to.

Most sexually transmitted diseases can be cured. Only AIDS cannot be cured. And in most cases, AIDS causes death. Herpes cannot be "cured," but it is treatable. With treatment, the symptoms of herpes can be lessened.

What Is a Disease?

A disease is something that makes a person sick. When a person is sick, the body changes. This makes someone feel ill. Sometimes many parts of the body stop working as they should. This can cause death.

Diseases can be caused by different kinds of germs. A germ is a tiny invader in the body. It comes in many different forms. It gets into the body many different ways. And when a germ is inside the body, it can cause trouble.

Germs come in many different forms. Some germs are bacteria. Bacteria are found almost everywhere. Many bacteria do not harm humans. There are bacteria in the air we breathe and the water we drink. There are even bacteria in our bodies. Some bacteria cause disease in humans. Food poisoning, for example, is caused by bacteria.

Other germs are fungi or parasites. Fungi are plant-like organisms. A mushroom is a fungus. Some fungi are very tiny. Some of the tiny fungi can cause disease and irritation to humans.

Athlete's foot is caused by a fungus. Human parasites are tiny animals that attach themselves to the human body. They use the human body as "food." They live off the materials in the body. Some parasites can be seen easily by the naked eye. Crabs (lice) are a parasite.

Viruses are also a kind of germ. A virus is something that gets into the cells of the body. The cells are among the smallest parts of a human body. All our body parts are made up of billions of cells. A virus attacks the cells and makes them act differently. They cannot perform their normal jobs.

A cold is caused by a virus. The "flu" (short for influenza) is also a virus. When you get sick with these diseases you have a virus inside you. You begin to feel ill because your body is suffering from the invasion by the virus. The symptoms you get— cough, fever, and aches—are all because of the invading virus that is attacking your cells.

Many of the diseases we will talk about are caused by bacteria and viruses.

Venereal disease and sexually transmitted diseases are called contagious diseases. Contagious means you can catch something from another person. They are sexually transmitted diseases because you catch them by having sex with another person who has the disease. This means having sex involving the penis, the vagina, the rectum, or the mouth.

Contagious diseases are serious and scary. They can spread very fast. One person can spread the disease to hundreds or thousands of other people. Here's an example: One infected person has sex with ten people. Then each of those people has sex with ten other people. That means that 101 people have been exposed to the disease. What if each of those people has sex with ten people? Then 1,110 people will be exposed. And all because of *one* infected person.

How Can STDs Be Prevented?

When and if you decide to have sex, the best way to prevent STDs is to follow responsible sexual behavior. This is commonly referred to as "safer sex." Safer sex generally means using condoms. Condoms are rubber casings that slip over the erect penis before sex. They prevent direct genital contact between partners. Without direct genital contact, the chance of giving someone a disease is much smaller. Condoms are also a very effective form of birth control. Other birth control items, such as diaphragms, foam, and suppositories, can protect females partially from STDs. They can also protect males from certain diseases. Contraceptive jelly and "the pill" do not prevent STDs.

Safer sex also means knowing about your partner's past sexual behavior. This is important because the people your partner has had sex with can have an effect on your health.

How Common Are STDs?

It is estimated that more than 1.5 million people get a venereal disease each year. Teenagers form a big part of that number. About 2,000 teens get syphilis or gonorrhea every day. Half the people who have STDs are under 25 years old. Sexually transmitted diseases, as you can see, are very common. They are common among teens because "safer sex" is not common enough.

Most STDs can be treated and cured if they are found early. Many people allow their disease to go without treatment for long periods of time. Many people are too embarrassed to seek health care. And many people do not know what the signs are. But these people are taking a very great risk. They are risking their health and maybe even their lives.

Summary

1. Sexually transmitted diseases (STDs or venereal diseases) are catching. They are spread by sexual contact including the penis, vagina, rectum, and mouth.
2. STDs are very dangerous if left untreated.
3. Most STDs can be cured if treated early. AIDS cannot be cured at all.
4. "Safer sex" greatly reduces the chances of giving or getting a sexually transmitted disease. Safer sex means wearing condoms. It also means knowing your partner's past sexual history.

Chapter 2

Some Facts About The Human Body

STDs are transmitted through sex. It is important to know how the human sex organs work. Often it is the sexual organs that show signs of an STD.

Different parts of the body are called organs. Every organ in the body is made up of tissue. And all tissue is made up of millions of cells. Cells, as we learned, are parts of the body that can be infected by different kinds of germs.

The Male Sex Organs

Some male sex organs are outside the body and some are inside. Outside are the penis and the testicles (or testes). The testes are in a sac called the scrotum. The testes produce sperm. Sperm are in semen (see-men), the male fertilizing liquid.

FEMALE REPRODUCTIVE SYSTEM

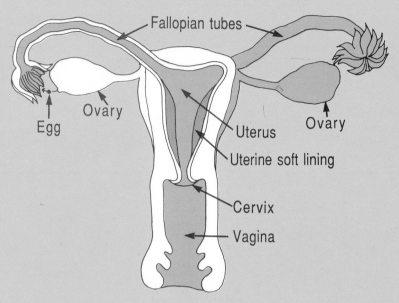

Fallopian tubes

Ovary

Egg

Uterus

Uterine soft lining

Cervix

Vagina

Ovary

MALE REPRODUCTIVE SYSTEM

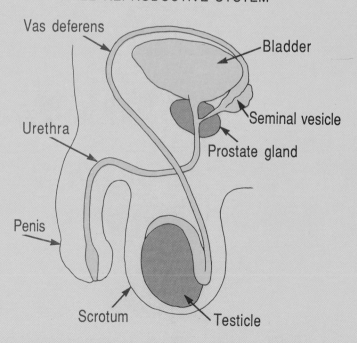

Vas deferens

Bladder

Urethra

Seminal vesicle

Prostate gland

Penis

Scrotum

Testicle

Males with an STD usually pass the disease through the penis. Usually, the bacteria are present in a tube inside the penis. When the erect penis is stimulated, it releases the semen in a series of muscular spasms called ejaculation. The bacteria are passed through the penis with the fluid that contains the sperm.

The Female Sex Organs

The external female sex organ is the clitoris. The clitoris becomes stimulated during sexual activity. The clitoris is located in front of the vagina. The vagina is the passage that leads to the uterus (womb). The fallopian tubes come out from either side of the uterus. An ovary is at the end of each tube. Each month one of the ovaries produces a mature egg cell. The egg then bursts out of the ovary and into a fallopian tube. When the egg is in the tube, it may be fertilized by a sperm. If it is not fertilized, the egg will be flushed out of the body through menstruation (the menstrual "period"). If the egg is fertilized by a sperm, it will attach itself to the wall of the uterus and begin to grow. It will become an embryo (em-bree-o). Then it will become a fetus (feet-us). Finally, it will be ready to be born as a baby.

The Effects of Sexual Intercourse

During sex there is usually an exchange of bodily fluids. The transmission involves a penis and a vagina, or a rectum, or a mouth. As we have heard, an infected person can pass a sexually transmitted germ to a partner. The germ can be passed through close bodily contact or exchange of bodily fluids. Kissing also exchanges a bodily fluid, saliva. But kissing is not usually very dangerous. Kissing may be dangerous if one person has an STD infection in their mouth or throat.

Ways to Reduce the Risks

1. Make it a habit to use condoms: Using condoms is smart. Condoms perform two very important jobs. They greatly reduce the chance of giving someone a sexually transmitted disease. And they greatly reduce the chance of pregnancy.

Some people do not want to "bother" with using condoms. A condom must be put on an erect penis, one that is stimulated. For some people this means "stopping at a bad time." Many people do not want to interrupt their lovemaking in order to put on a condom. Many people are probably embarrassed by it, too. And some people are afraid that their partner will lose interest in lovemaking if they stop even briefly. But a condom will keep you from getting AIDS, or getting another disease. And it will prevent pregnancy. PREVENTION IS WORTH A TINY INTERRUPTION!

Many people don't know that they
have a sexually transmitted disease.
They may infect several sexual
partners.

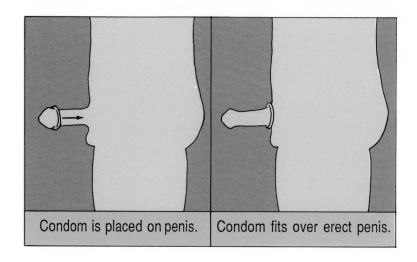

| Condom is placed on penis. | Condom fits over erect penis. |

Condoms can be bought in many places. Since AIDS has become a serious worry, condoms are more widely placed. In addition to being sold in any drugstore, condoms can often be found at school health clinics, Planned Parenthood offices, your doctor's office, at gas stations, and in public rest rooms.

Important note: Never use a condom from an open wrapper. And never use a condom more than once.

2. Know about your partner: As we saw in Chapter One, STDs can spread very easily. Sex with someone who has had sex with many other people in a short period of time is a risk. Each person that your partner has had sex with increases the chances that they have a disease. And that increases your chances of getting it.

3. Be aware of your body: Look carefully at your body. Know what your body looks like. Pay attention to how you feel and how you look. Keep an eye out for any change in what your body looks like or how it works. Pay attention to changes in your body. They could be signs of an STD.

4. Be aware of your partner's body: Watch for any strange changes in appearance or any other problems you may see.

Summary

1. Male organs are the penis, the testes, and the scrotum.
2. Female organs are the clitoris, vagina, and the uterus (womb).
3. STDs are transmitted by the exchange of bodily fluids and by close body contact during sexual activity.
4. There are ways to reduce the risks of getting an STD. An important way is always to use a condom. Another way is to remember that each different partner increases the chances of getting an STD.

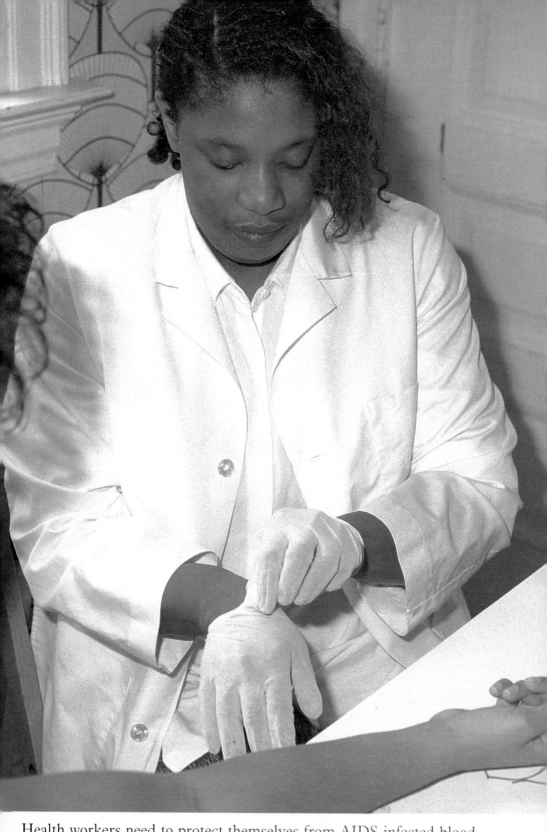

Health workers need to protect themselves from AIDS-infected blood.

Chapter 3

AIDS: The Greatest Fear

Ms. Margaret Lytton
Guidance Counselor
Warrenbrook High School

Dear Ms. Lytton,

Thank you for talking with me yesterday at school.
What you told me about AIDS was very helpful. Now
that I know about it, I'm not as scared. I was most re-
lieved to hear that you can't get AIDS from casual contact. Before I knew that I was scared all the time. I was
frightened that someone might touch me and I would
get AIDS.

I know how serious AIDS is in the United States. I
know many people have already died from it. It is easy
to be scared by it. That is why it is important for
everyone to know the facts. And now I'll be able to tell
my friends the facts too.

Thanks again,

Roberto

You have probably heard a lot about AIDS lately. That is because AIDS has become an epidemic. That means it is a very serious disease that has infected many people in a very short time. Ten years ago, only two cases of AIDS were known. Nine years ago only seven cases were reported. By 1983 there were about 2,950 people with AIDS in the United States. By 1989 the figure had grown to over 100,000.

Fighting AIDS has become a national goal. Finding a cure for the disease has also become a major aim for doctors and scientists around the world. Many people now know how AIDS is transmitted. They also know about "safer sex." AIDS has made people more aware of other sexually transmitted diseases too. It is good that more people have become educated about STDs in recent years.

What Is AIDS?

AIDS stands for Acquired Immune Deficiency Syndrome. That's a medical way of saying that the AIDS virus attacks the body's immune system. The immune system is the body's system for fighting disease and infection.

When an invading virus or germ (like a cold or the flu) enters the body, the immune system immediately begins to fight it. White blood cells try to kill the cells that have been invaded by the virus. They try to stop them from multiplying. If the white blood cells cannot kill enough of the virus cells, the virus will take over. The person will be sick.

The AIDS virus enters the body through the bloodstream. Almost always, it enters when bodily fluids are shared between two people. This can happen when an infected person shares a needle with a person who is not infected. Or it can happen when an infected person has sex with a person who is not infected. During sex, the AIDS virus is transported in the semen (sperm-carrying fluid) of the male. The semen transmits the virus into the body of the partner by way of the vagina, the rectum, or the mouth.

Once the virus is inside, it begins to grow and multiply. Then it attacks the immune system. Doctors do not know everything about how the immune system is destroyed. And they do not know how to stop the AIDS virus from multiplying. They do know, however, that once the virus has started to do its work, the body will soon lose its ability to fight disease. Once the immune system is destroyed, the victim cannot fight off even the most common viruses and germs. It is only a matter of time until the victim's body cannot function. Then the person will die.

What Are the Symptoms?

Often, the symptoms of AIDS take a while (even years) to appear. People can be carrying the virus but appear to be healthy. Sometimes they can appear healthy for up to seven years while carrying the virus. This period is called the "incubation period." It is the time when the virus is "growing" inside the body. All STDs have an incubation period.

There are many symptoms of AIDS. Patients may have some or all of the symptoms. Each body's immune system will resist AIDS in a different way. And each body will react by showing symptoms in a different way. The most common symptoms of AIDS are:

○ very bad fatigue
○ swollen lymph glands
○ rapid weight loss
○ stubborn cough
○ coated tongue and throat
○ unexplained bleeding
○ frequent fever
○ night sweats
○ purple skin tumors
○ bumps, rashes, or other strange developments on the skin
○ easy bruising
○ trouble recovering from common illness, such as cold or flu

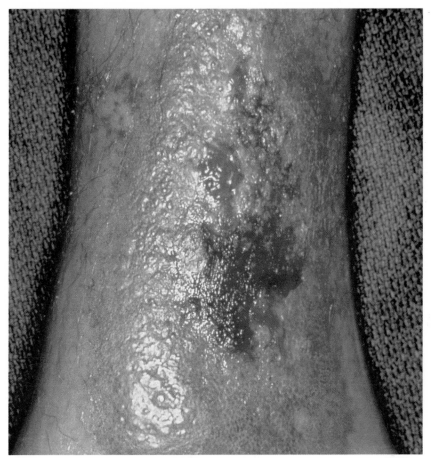

Kaposi's sarcoma is a kind of skin cancer often seen in AIDS patients.

Who Gets AIDS?

As we have learned, AIDS is passed through the blood and certain body fluids. Anyone can get AIDS. But you only get AIDS by close contact with the blood or bodily fluids of a person with the AIDS virus.

People who can get AIDS without having sexual contact are newborn babies, intravenous drug users (people who use needles to take drugs), and people who had blood transfusions before 1985. A baby can be infected if a parent carries AIDS. A baby has a 50 percent chance of being born with AIDS if a parent carries the virus. People who had blood transfusions before 1985 run a small risk too. This is because before 1985 AIDS had not yet been identified and labeled as so serious. Before 1985, blood was not tested for AIDS before it was used for transfusion. Like any other disease, AIDS is most common in large cities. That is because cities have more people per square mile than country areas.

It is important to remember that you cannot get AIDS through casual (cahs-u-el) contact. You cannot get AIDS from touching a person with AIDS. You cannot get AIDS from the air. And you can't get AIDS from a mosquito bite.

Today's Research

Experts think that more than 1.5 million Americans may carry the AIDS virus today. People may carry the virus and not be sick. These people are called "carriers." Carriers do not appear sick. But they can transmit the virus to others.

Much time and money are being given to research. Today, doctors and scientists still cannot prevent AIDS from killing its victims. Some drugs, such as AZT, can help to lengthen the lives of some patients. But these drugs cannot cure AIDS.

How to Protect and Prevent

Protection and prevention are necessary and quite easy. Like other STDs, AIDS is transmitted through the blood and body fluids. There are no fail-proof ways to prevent STDs. Some ways are better than others. The best way to prevent transmission during sex is to use condoms. It is also wise to know about your partner's past sexual activity. If he or she has had sex with a great many people in a short period of time, the chances are increased that they have been exposed. And, finally, one should never share a needle or use illegal drugs.

Summary

1. AIDS is an epidemic. That means it is serious and spreading out of control.

2. AIDS is a virus. It attacks the body's immune system.

3. AIDS is transmitted through the blood or semen. It can be transmitted by sex using the penis, vagina, rectum, and mouth. It can also be transmitted by sharing needles.

4. AIDS is deadly.

5. The risk of getting AIDS can be reduced by using condoms and by practicing "safer sex."

Sores on the lip might be a sign of a venereal disease.

Chapter 4

Syphilis: The Well-Disguised Danger

Dear Joan,

I'm sorry I haven't written in a while. I was a little upset last week. Something happened that has never happened to me before. I noticed a red sore on my lower lip. It didn't hurt but it looked terrible.

Of course, I told Ted right away. And we stopped having sex right away. I went to the doctor immediately. She said it looked like syphilis. I had a test done. It was syphilis. I got very worried. But the doctor told me that it would be cured in a very short time. All I needed was some medicine called penicillin. The doctor also said it was very good that I came right away. Evidently, it is best to treat these things as soon as possible.

Ted also went to his doctor. He had syphilis too. Anyway, we're both feeling fine now. And I look forward to seeing you next weekend.

Best,
Karen

Syphilis is caused by a tiny germ called a *spirochete* (spy-ro-keet). Spirochetes are bacteria. They are very, very small and can live almost anywhere in the body.

Syphilis is also contagious (catching). That means one person gets it from another person who has it. Syphilis is a venereal disease. It is transmitted only through sexual contact.

Syphilis has a long incubation period. That means it takes a long time for it to grow and be seen. The incubation period for syphilis is three weeks to three months.

After incubation a sore appears at the infected area. The sore is infectious for as long as it can be seen. The spirochetes are in the sore. The spirochetes carry the disease.

A syphilis sore is called a chancre (shanker). A chancre can look like a cut or a rash. A person can become infected with syphilis by having direct contact with an open sore. The sore may be in the mouth, vagina, rectum, or on the penis of an infected person. This contact happens during sex with an infected person. During sex, the man's penis comes in contact with the vagina, rectum, or mouth of his partner. These are usually the organs that have the syphilis sores. And that is when the spirochetes (germs) move into the body of the healthy person.

The Stages of Syphilis

A chancre sore will develop on the part of the body where the infection was passed. This is called the *primary lesion of syphilis.* Usually this sore will look terrible. It may look red and it may be wet. But this sore does not usually hurt. It just looks bad.

Sometimes the primary sore will be easy to see. It may be on the penis. But many syphilis sores are not easy to see. They can be inside the vagina, or under the foreskin of the penis. They can also be under the tongue or inside the rectum. Often, the infected person doesn't see the sore.

After a few weeks, the chancre disappears. When a chancre (or sore) heals there is a feeling of relief. Often the infected person will feel as if the syphilis has "gone away." But it has not gone away. It is just "hiding" inside the body until later.

If the sore has disappeared and the syphilis is still not treated, the disease gets more serious. It enters the *secondary stage.* The secondary stage is anywhere from six weeks to six months after the infection began.

In the secondary stage, the spirochetes have multiplied throughout the whole body. The symptoms can take different forms. Most symptoms are in the mucous membranes and the skin. The mucous membranes are the soft linings inside the body cavities, like the nose and mouth. A rash can now break out on the skin. It can be

everywhere on the body. It is often on the palms of
the hands and the soles of the feet. Patches of hair
can fall out too.

When these symptoms appear, it means the
person is very contagious. A partner will get
syphilis from the person. The symptoms can last
weeks. Eventually they go away. But even when
they go away, the syphilis stays.

Latent Syphilis

After the second stage disappears, the person has
latent syphilis. Latent means hidden. A person with
latent syphilis may no longer have any symptoms.
But a blood test would still show the disease.

Most people are not infectious after they have
had syphilis for one year. They will no longer give
the disease to others. But if syphilis is not treated
for a long time it will cause more serious damage.
Untreated patients can develop brain damage. The
spirochetes will destroy the tissues in the brain.
This often causes insanity that cannot be cured.

There are other symptoms of untreated syphilis.
Spinal cord damage and paralysis can occur. Many
victims lose their ability to walk and also to see.
These are all results of the spirochetes slowly
damaging the tissues of organs.

Syphilis and Pregnancy

It is very dangerous for a pregnant woman to have
syphilis. A pregnant woman with syphilis will pass

the disease to her child. Syphilis in newborn infants can cause deformities and even death.

How Is Syphilis Treated?

Treatment for syphilis is simple. Especially if the disease is seen and treated early.

Syphilis can be treated and cured by penicillin. If a patient is allergic to penicillin, another medicine can be used. Usually that is all that is needed to cure syphilis.

Syphilis Today

Syphilis is still a major health problem in the United States. The only way to control syphilis is to reduce the number of people who are infected. And that can only happen when more people practice "safer sex."

Summary

1. Syphilis is caused by tiny bacteria called spirochetes. They get into the bloodstream when a healthy person has sexual contact with a person who has syphilis.
2. There are three stages of syphilis. First is the primary stage. Then there is the secondary stage. Then syphilis becomes latent (hidden).
3. Syphilis can be treated and cured with penicillin or other medicines.
4. If not treated, syphilis causes serious damage to many organs in the body.

If one partner infects the other with an STD, both partners must be treated by a doctor.

Chapter 5

Gonorrhea and Chlamydia: Growing Problems

Dear Danny,

I'm sorry I yelled at you last night. I know this whole thing isn't your fault. You had no idea that what you had was gonorrhea. I shouldn't have blamed you for "burning me."

It's both our faults, really. We should have used a condom all the time. I think that once or twice without a condom was enough to give the bacteria to me.

I think we should both go to the doctor's office together tomorrow. Will you come with me? That way we can get treated together.

Talk to you tonight,

Love,

Maria

Gonorrhea and chlamydia are common STDs. Most people have heard of gonorrhea. But many people do not know about chlamydia. Chlamydia can cause serious problems if it is not treated. But it can be treated.

Many people make a joke of gonorrhea. They call it many other names. They call it "the clap," or "the drip." But gonorrhea is a serious disease. It should be treated as soon as possible.

What Causes Gonorrhea?

Gonorrhea is caused by the bacteria called *Neisseria gonorrhea*. These bacteria cannot live outside the body. They live in the mucous membranes. Those are the soft linings inside organs like the eyelids, the mouth, the rectum, the penis, or the vagina.

It is not true that you can get gonorrhea by casual contact. You cannot get it from a doorknob or a toilet seat. You can't get it by a handshake or through a break in the skin. The ways for it to pass from one person to another is through sexual activity or childbirth.

Gonorrhea in Men

When a healthy man has sex with a partner who has gonorrhea, the bacteria enter the part of the body used during sex—the penis, mouth, or rectum. Gonorrhea is commonly found in the

penis. The gonorrhea bacteria enter the urethra
through the opening at the head of the penis. The
urethra is a tube in the penis. The tube carries the
man's sperm and his urine. In the urethra, the
bacteria start to multiply. Each ten to fifteen
minutes they double in number. Within hours
there are millions. This incubation (growing)
period can last up to 28 days. The usual incubation
period is one to ten days. Symptoms usually appear
in three to five days. The body tries to fight the
infection. But the white blood cells are quickly
outnumbered. The dead white blood cells and the
bacteria form pus. The pus collects in the infected
area and begins to ooze.

After incubation, the symptoms appear. There is
a burning feeling when urinating. Pus oozes from
the penis. This is when most people seek help.
Gonorrhea should be treated before these
symptoms appear. Otherwise, it can be even more
serious.

Bacteria will travel from the urethra to other
male sex organs, the testicles. Pus in these organs
can leave scar tissue. The scar tissue can cause a
man to become sterile. That means he is unable to
have children. Untreated gonorrhea can also cause
arthritis and heart trouble.

A man is just as likely to have gonorrhea as a
woman. And a man can give gonorrhea to a woman
during sex. A woman can also give it to a man.

When persons are infected, chances are they will infect a partner during sex.

Often, one partner will blame the other for "giving" him or her gonorrhea. This attitude is unfair. When two people have sex, they are both responsible for what happens. Some people know they have an STD. They have sex without telling their partner about the STD. This is never fair to the partner. STDs are serious. And both partners should know of anything that may happen if they have sex.

Gonorrhea in Women

When a healthy woman has sex with a partner who has gonorrhea, the bacteria enter through the part of the body used during sex, the vagina, the rectum, or the mouth. Most often the bacteria enter through the vagina. When they enter through the vagina the bacteria are placed in the cervix. The cervix is the opening of the uterus. It is hidden from sight.

Sometimes the infection will cause a mild burning during urination. Sometimes there will be pus from the vagina. But it is most common for no symptoms to be seen at all.

When the bacteria travel to the other sex organs the infection is more serious. The bacteria will settle in the uterus and/or fallopian tubes. These are important organs for reproduction. When these organs are infected there is pus inside. This pus builds up and causes swelling and pain. There can also be pain in the belly and fever. If gonorrhea is not treated, the woman may become sterile. That means she will not be able to have children.

A pregnant woman may become infected with gonorrhea. If the disease is not cured, the baby can pick up the bacteria during birth. The pus will get into the baby's eyes. This can cause blindness.

Gonorrhea is dangerous for a pregnant woman. It can cause blindness in the baby.

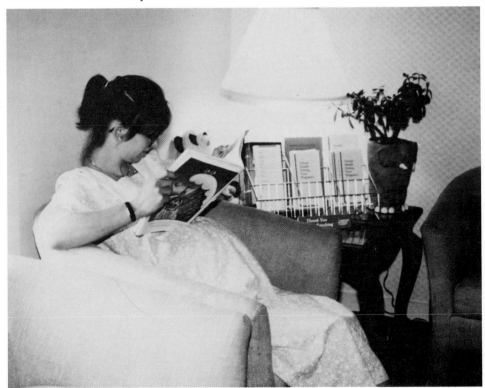

How Is Gonorrhea Treated?

Gonorrhea bacteria can be detected under a microscope. A pus sample will show the bacteria.

In many states, gonorrhea is no longer treated with penicillin. That is because some kinds of bacteria are not killed by penicillin. Patients in these states are treated with other medication that can kill the bacteria.

Chlamydia and Treatment

Anyone with gonorrhea is now treated for chlamydia at the same time. Chlamydia is another STD. It is caused by bacteria called *Chlamydia trachomatis*. The bacteria are transmitted by direct contact with the genitals, rectum, or mouth during sex.

Symptoms (signs) of a chlamydia infection may appear within a week of exposure. Sometimes it can take up to a month for symptoms to appear. The symptoms can be very difficult to spot. About 80 percent of women do not have any symptoms that they can see or feel. The seriousness of chlamydia will only be felt when the infection advances. The disease can affect a woman's ability to have a child.

Many men will not notice symptoms either.

The symptoms of chlamydia are like those of gonorrhea. They include the following: For women, the infection can cause discharge from the vagina. Women may also have a "burning" feeling when urinating. Some women may also have lower pain in their sides, a low-grade fever, and bleeding in between periods. Men may experience burning during urination and discharge from the penis. Burning and itching around the penis may also occur. Sometimes the testicles will swell up and there will be a low-grade fever.

If chlamydia is not treated it can cause some serious health problems. The infection can be treated with antibiotics. It is becoming a very common STD.

Summary

1. Gonorrhea is caused by bacteria called *Neisseria gonorrhea*. They cannot live outside the body. They are only transmitted through sex.
2. You cannot get gonorrhea or chlamydia casually—from a handshake or a toilet seat.
3. Untreated gonorrhea and untreated chlamydia can cause serious problems. They can cause men and women to become sterile. They can also harm newborn babies.
4. Gonorrhea and chlamydia can usually be prevented by "safer sex." Gonorrhea and chlamydia can also be prevented by not having sex with someone who has them.

Support groups can help people deal with diseases like herpes.

Chapter 6

Genital Herpes: One of Many Herpes

Dear Kim,

Thanks for your letter telling me why you haven't called me. I thought it was something more serious. I thought you had been in an accident or something.

Now I understand why you didn't want to date me anymore. I know you were afraid. But herpes doesn't mean you have to lock yourself away forever. It only means you and your partner have to be careful. A partner can only catch it from you at certain times. And there are precautions we can use to be safer.

I have grown to love you. And I'm not willing to let that go down the drain just because of this. You're right, it is a problem. But it can be dealt with. The most important thing is that you told me. And I understand. And I don't think any less of you because of it. I don't think you're "dirty." I know that has nothing to do with it.

I understand. And I hope you'll answer my next call so I can tell you in person. See you soon.

Love,

Cal

There many different kinds of herpes. All herpes are caused by viruses.

Viruses are too small to be seen with the naked eye. Even a light microscope cannot see them. Some viruses can be seen with a super-powerful microscope called an electron microscope.

Viruses enter the body through the nose, mouth, or skin. Measles, mumps, chicken pox, influenza (the flu), and the common cold are all caused by viruses.

One thing is puzzling about viruses. They do not look or act like living cells. Most cells are "alive." They perform functions such as taking in food, digesting food, and getting rid of waste. They also reproduce. Scientists do not consider viruses to be "alive." That is because they do not take in food or digest food. All they do is reproduce. And they only "come alive" when they are inside another cell.

Not all living cells can be attacked by viruses. The host cell (a cell that a virus lives in) must have a special membrane. The virus needs to attach itself to the membrane. Once the virus is attached, it invades the living cell. The virus uses the cell's materials to reproduce itself. The virus takes over the living cell completely.

The virus reproduces itself many times in the first host cell. Soon the cell bursts open and

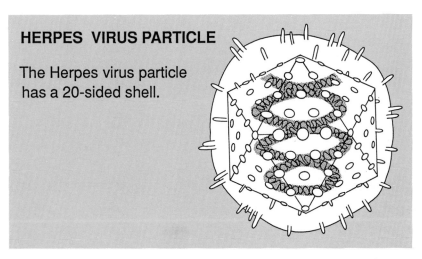

HERPES VIRUS PARTICLE

The Herpes virus particle
has a 20-sided shell.

releases virus particles into the body. These viruses
invade more cells. And each of these cells then
hosts the growth of more virus particles.

The Herpes Virus Group

Herpes in Greek means "to creep." The virus was
named this because it can hide in the body for a
long time without being detected. Then, without
warning, it can come out and cause serious
problems.

Five Types of Herpes

There are five kinds of herpes virus. Not all herpes
viruses are sexually transmitted. One causes
chicken pox and "shingles" in adults, another
causes mononucleosis ("mono"), and another
causes cytomegalovirus (CMV). Herpes simplex 1
(HSV-1) causes cold sores and blisters, usually on
the mouth, and Herpes simplex 2 (HSV-2) causes
genital herpes.

HSV-1 is transmitted by kissing or touching someone who has a "cold sore" or is "shedding." Shedding means transmitting diseased cells without having a sore or blister. The virus can stay inside the body for a long time. It will usually appear during times of stress and low body resistance. HSV-1 can sometimes be passed by sexual contact and is often mixed with HSV-2.

HSV-2 is venereal herpes. It is also called genital herpes. It is a sexually transmitted disease (STD). HSV-2 can enter the body through the mucous membranes of the mouth, rectum, penis, or vagina. Herpes sores will then appear at the site of the infection.

The symptoms are usually the worst when a person is initially infected. The person may have a burning and itching at the sores. There may also be numbness (lack of feeling), headache, and fever. Often the person has muscle aches and swollen glands. Usually a person also has poor appetite and a lack of energy.

Herpes symptoms can occur again later. Once the herpes virus is in the body it does not leave. It is there for life. Herpes is not like gonorrhea or syphilis. There is no known cure for HSV-2. Usually, the symptoms in later outbreaks are not as bad as they are the first time. The later outbreaks can have sores. All outbreaks are uncomfortable.

Herpes can also cause worry for those who have it. They can worry about when the symptoms will come out again. They can also worry about giving the disease to others. But genital herpes is usually contagious only at certain times.

Experts believe that one out of every five American adults may get HSV-2 each year. It is estimated that 50 to 150 million people are already infected.

Summary

1. Herpes is a virus.
2. There are five kinds of herpes viruses. Herpes simplex 2 (HSV-2) is genital herpes.
3. Herpes (both HSV-1—cold sores—and HSV-2) can be transmitted by sexual activity.
4. Symptoms of genital herpes can be very painful. They include sores, aching muscles and joints, and swelling and pain in the genitals.
5. There is treatment for genital herpes but there is no cure.
6. Genital herpes can be prevented. Avoid sex with partners who have open sores or are shedding. Using condoms greatly reduces the risk of transmission.

Responsible sex involves open discussion and honesty with your
sexual partner.

Chapter 7

Genital Warts

Genital warts are also called venereal warts. They are fast becoming one of the most common STDs in the United States. About 1 million people get genital warts each year.

Venereal warts are growths that appear on the parts of the body that are used during sex. They include the penis, the vagina, the anus, and the back of the throat. The warts are caused by viruses. And the viruses spread only through sexual contact.

Often, the warts look harmless. But they should be treated as soon as possible. They can multiply and spread very quickly. And the longer they grow, the harder it is to get rid of them.

The viruses that cause warts are spread during sex. Just like all STDs. Warts might appear a few weeks after exposure. Or they might take months to appear. But just because you cannot see the warts does not mean they are not there. A person can be infected and pass the virus on without knowing it.

The warts usually look like tiny cauliflowers. They are bumpy. But sometimes they are flat. Some warts are so small that they can only be seen under a microscope. They can sometimes cause itching. But they do not usually cause pain.

The best way to make sure you do not have genital warts is to see a doctor. Have her check any strange growths, sores, or skin changes you may have. Sores or growths near or on your penis, vagina, or anus are very important. If you do have warts, the doctor can remove them. Small warts can be treated with a liquid that dissolves them. Larger warts can be removed by freezing them. These methods are not expensive. And they do not hurt.

There is one more very important thing to do if you find out that you have genital warts. Tell your sex partner(s). Chances are they will have the virus too.

Summary

1. Genital warts are a very common STD in the United States. They are growths that appear on the body near the sex organs, or the mouth or rectum.
2. Warts should be treated as soon as possible.

Conclusion

There are other sexually transmitted diseases. Many can be just as serious as those we have discussed. But those diseases are less common than the ones we have learned about.

Some sexually transmitted problems are not as serious as herpes, or gonorrhea, or syphilis. But they are still problems. Pubic lice can be shared during sexual or close contact. And so can scabies. Scabies are tiny "mite-like" creatures that live on the skin. The symptoms of these two problems are similar. Usually they cause rashes and itching. They can be treated with a medicated shampoo or lotion.

The Teen and Sex: Special Problems

Teens have an especially hard time with their feelings about sex. Puberty and adolescence are very confusing times. Teens have sexual urges that they have never had before. Sometimes teens ignore the fact that sex requires some precaution.

Teenagers can get information or advice from parents or counselors.

Most teens experience emotional changes during puberty. New sexual desires make teens anxious. Teens feel that changes in their bodies are scary and embarrassing. The thought of sex can be both exciting and scary too. Often teens find it hard to handle the responsibilities of sexual activity. They use an excuse. They say it is "too hard" for them to think about "safer sex" when they are unsure about sex.

The most important thing for teens to remember is *responsibility*. That means being grown-up about what you do. It means remembering that what you do today can affect what happens tomorrow. It means thinking about the risks of sex. And making decisions.

What we have learned in this book can make all teens more responsible. Let's review some of the most important facts:

1. It is most important to take good care of yourself. That means paying attention to your body. And seeing a doctor or nurse if it is needed.
2. Some STDs can be cured.
3. Some STDs cannot be cured.
4. It is always best to treat STDs as early as possible.
5. The risk of getting an STD is greatly reduced by "safer sex." That means using condoms.
6. You can reduce risks by knowing some background about your sexual partners. Reducing the number of partners you have will also reduce risks.

This book has shown you how serious STDs can be. And it has told you how important it is to prevent them, and that prevention is not very difficult.

Maybe you have even thought about things you can do to be more careful about sex. And you can probably see one thing quite clearly: A little bit of prevention can save you a great deal of trouble later.

Glossary—*Explaining New Words*

acute stage   Very serious stage.

AIDS   Acquired Immune Deficiency Syndrome, a sexually transmitted virus.

antibodies   Organisms made by the immune system that fight infection and disease in body.

cervix   Inside vagina, the opening of the uterus.

communicable   Contagious, passed from one person to another.

condom   Contraceptive, a rubber casing that goes over the erect penis.

contagious   Transmitted from one person to another.

cytomegalovirus   Herpes virus passed to newborn babies by the mother.

embryo   Fertilized egg in early stages of development.

fallopian tubes   Tubes that carry eggs from the ovaries to the uterus.

fatigue   Tiredness.

fertilize   To start life.

fetus   Fertilized egg in later stages of development.

fungus   Tiny plant growths that grow on the body.

genital herpes   Sexually transmitted virus.

gonorrhea   Sexually transmitted bacteria.

homosexual   "Gay," person who has sex with another of the same sex.

immune system   Fights infection in the body.

incubation   Growth time.

infectious   Contagious, able to be passed from one person to another.

latent   Hidden.

menstruation   "Period," monthly female bleeding.

metropolitan   City.

mucuous membrane   Soft lining inside organs like mouth, vagina, and rectum.

ovaries   Contain the eggs in a female.

paralysis   Inability to move.

pelvis   Lower abdominal area, near the genitals.

penis   Male external sex organ.

puberty   The beginning of sexual feelings and growth of sexual organs.

pus   White liquid that collects in sores and infected areas.

rectum   Anus.

"safer sex"   Sex with condoms to prevent transmitting STDs.

scrotum   Sac that holds the testes (testicles).

semen   Liquid from penis containing sperm.

shedding   Most infectious period.

sperm   Male fertilizing organisms.

spirochete   Germ that causes syphilis.

STDs   Sexually transmitted diseases.

syphilis   A sexually transmitted disease.

testes   Testicles.

testicles   Testes, produce sperm in the male.

transfusion (blood)   Putting one person's blood into another person.

tumors   Bumps or lumps of tissues that form in the body.

urethra   Tube that carries male's sperm and urine through penis.

uterus   Womb, gives nourishment to a fetus when woman is pregnant.

vagina   Female opening to sexual organs.

VD   Venereal disease.

venereal diseases   STDs, diseases transmitted by sex.

virus   Organism that invades the cells of the body.

womb   Uterus, sac in which the fetus develops.

Where To Get Help

AIDS Action Council
Federation of AIDS-Related
   Organizations
729 Eighth Street, SE
Suite 200
Washington, DC 20003
Phone: (202) 547-3101

Herpes Resource Center
P.O. Box 100
Palo Alto, CA 94302
Telephone: (415) 328-7710

American Foundation for the Prevention of Venereal Disease
799 Broadway, Suite 638
New York, NY 10003
Telephone: (212) 759-2069

Birth Control Institute
1242 Lincoln Ave., Suite 7–10
Anaheim, CA 92805
Telephone: (714) 956-4630

Public Health Service, Center for Disease Control
U.S. Public Health Service
1600 Clifton Road, NE
Atlanta, GA 30333
Telephone: (404) 329-3534
Hotline Phone: 1-800-442-0366

National Coalition of Gay Sexually Transmitted Disease Services
P.O. Box 239
Milwaukee, WI 53201
Telephone: (414) 277-7671

For Further Reading

Barlow, David. *Sexually Transmitted Diseases: The Facts,* New York: Oxford University Press, 1979. A study of the causes, symptoms, and cures for STDs. Part of the "The Facts" series, illustrated.

Connell, Elizabeth B., and Tatum, Howard J. *Sexually Transmitted Diseases: Diagnosis and Treatment,* New York: Creative Infomatics, 1985. How to identify symptoms and treat STDs safely and effectively.

Edwards, Gabrielle. *Coping with Venereal Disease,* New York: Rosen Publishing, 1985. Covers human reproductive systems, the history of each disease, statistics, and contains a question & answer wrap-up. Illustrated.

Ulene, Art. *Safe Sex in a Dangerous World.* New York: Vintage Books, 1987. Prevention methods for STDs with discussions about responsibility and other sexual behaviors.

Zinner, Stephen. *How to Protect Yourself from STDs,* New York: Summit Books, 1986. A handbook of prevention methods, as well as a discussion of treatments.

Index

About the Author
Samuel G. Woods is a New York-based writer who specializes in writing for young adults. He currently works in Manhattan, where he also does freelance editing and photography.

About the Editor
Evan Stark is a well-known sociologist, educator, and therapist as well as a popular lecturer on women's and children's health issues. Dr. Stark was the Henry Rutgers Fellow at Rutgers University, an associate at the Institution for Social and Policy Studies at Yale University, and a Fulbright Fellow at the University of Essex. He is the author of many publications in the field of family relations and is the father of four children.

Acknowledgments and Photo Credits
Photographs by Stuart Rabinowitz; p. 7, 22, 49, Sonja Kalter

Design/Production: Blackbirch Graphics, Inc.
Cover Photograph: Charles Waldon